FIGHTING FORCES ON THE SEA

AMPHIBIOUS ASSAULT SHIPS

LYNN M. STONE

Rourke
Publishing LLC
Vero Beach, Florida 32964

www.rourkepublishing.com

PHOTO CREDITS: p. 24, 25 courtesy U.S. Department of Defense National Archives; other photos courtesy U.S. Navy

Title page: *LCACs can haul a heavy load at high speed, making them ideal for surprise amphibious assaults.*

Editor: Frank Sloan

          Library of Congress Cataloging-in-Publication Data

Stone, Lynn M.
  Amphibious assault ships / Lynn M. Stone.
      p. cm. -- (Fighting forces on the sea)
  Includes bibliographical references and index.
  ISBN 1-59515-460-4 (hardcover)

Printed in the USA

CG/CG

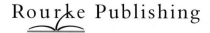

Rourke Publishing

www.rourkepublishing.com – sales@rourkepublishing.com
Post Office Box 3328, Vero Beach, FL 32964

1-800-394-7055

TABLE OF CONTENTS

AMPHIBIOUS ASSAULT SHIPS

Amphibious assault ships are big, broad-decked warships that look like low-carb aircraft carriers. Amphibious assault ships, designated LHDs and LHAs by the U.S. Navy, are most of a football field's length shorter than U.S. aircraft carriers. And although the big deck amphibs carry aircraft, the ships are designed for a much different purpose than the carriers.

▲
An amphibious assault ship with parked aircraft steams through the Mediterranean Sea.

A Marine Corps CH-46E helicopter lifts off from the flight deck of the amphibious assault ship USS Kearsarge.

An aircraft carrier is home for about 85 airplanes, most of them strike, or attack, aircraft, such as Tomcat, Hornet, and Super Hornet fighters. Normally, amphibious assault ships carry about 23 helicopters and only 6 attack aircraft. Furthermore, it is the amphibious assault ship's job to quickly and safely move U.S. Marines and their support equipment from ship to shore by landing craft and helicopter. It is this link between water and land, of course, that makes these ships amphibious.

The aircraft aboard amphibs are basically there to support Marines. Even the attack aircraft on an amphib, its AV-8B Harrier jets, are designed for close-in troop support, not for long-range bombing or combat with enemy jets.

"Assault" clearly means to attack, but do not confuse amphibious assault ships with actual attack ships—the **cruisers**, **destroyers**, and **frigates**. The big amphibs are only lightly armed. Their assault capability is not in their weaponry. Their assault capability is in the aircraft, mobile weaponry, and Marines that they transport.

Amphibious assault ships themselves are too big to go ashore, but they carry both the craft that ferry Marines ashore and the vehicles that move them about on land.

The Navy has two similar **classes** of amphibs, the *Wasp* class (LHD) and the *Tarawa* class (LHA). The *Tarawa*-class ships are the older of the two. They were introduced with the **commissioning** of the USS *Tarawa* (LHA 1) in 1976. There are five *Tarawa*-class ships currently in service.

The USS *Wasp* (LHD 1), commissioned in 1989, was the first ship of its class. It has since been joined by seven others, most recently the USS *Iwo Jima* (LHD 7) in 2001. She was the third LHD to have been designed with quarters for women. The eighth and final ship in the class will be the USS *Makin Island* (LHD 8), expected in 2006.

▲

The Tarawa-class amphibious assault ship USS Saipan
*(LHA 2) prepares to launch a CH-46 Sea Knight
helicopter and a CH-53 Super Stallion helicopter from its
flight deck.*

Slightly larger than their *Tarawa*-class cousins, the *Wasp* ships are the largest amphibious ships in the world. (The two classes have the same basic **hull** and engineering plant.) The newer *Wasp* class is an upgrade. It has an improved flight deck-elevator design and a larger **well deck**. It is also the first class of assault ships built to carry the AV-8B Harrier and the LCAC hovercraft.

The *Wasps* also accommodate the full range of Navy and Marine helicopters, conventional landing craft, and amphibious assault vehicles.

▲

The Wasp-class Kearsarge, *standing off the coast of Kuwait, sends an LCAC (Landing Cushion Air Craft) ashore with Marines and equipment.*

▲

An AV-8B II Harrier, a Marine close-support attack jet, lands on the flight deck of the amphibious assault ship Kearsage.

The cargo aboard an amphibious assault ship can support a Marine Expeditionary Unit of nearly 2,000 Marines. "Support" means housing the Marines, transporting them ashore, and assisting with firepower for their assault on a shore target.

Wasp class – LHD

Powerplant:
2 boilers, 2 geared steam turbines, 2 shafts; 70,000 total shaft horsepower

Length:
844 feet (253 meters)

Beam:
106 feet (32 meters)

Displacement (LHD 8):
41,772 tons (38,013 metric tons) fully loaded

Speed:
20+ knots (23.5 miles, 38 kilometers per hour)

Ship's company:
104 officers, 1,004 enlisted, and 1,894 Marines

Aircraft, depending upon mission:
12 CH-46 Sea Knight helicopters, 4 CH-53E Sea Stallion helicopters, 6 AV-8B Harrier attack jets, 3 UH-1N Huey helicopters, 4 AH-1W Super Cobra helicopters

Armament:
2 rolling airframe missile launchers, 2 Sea Sparrow missile launchers, 3 Phalanx Close-In Weapons Systems, 4 50-caliber machine guns, 4 25-millimeter MK 38 machine guns

Commissioning date, first ship:
1989

Tarawa class – LHA

Powerplant:
2 boilers, 2 geared steam turbines, 2 shafts; 70,000 total shaft horsepower

Length:
820 feet (250 meters)

Beam:
106 feet (32 meters)

Displacement:
39,400 tons (35,854 metric tons) fully loaded

Speed:
24 knots (27.6 miles, 44 kilometers per hour)

Aircraft, depending upon mission:
12 CH-46 Sea Knight helicopters, 4 CH-53 Sea Stallion helicopters, 6 AV-8B Harrier attack jets, 3 UH-1N Huey helicopters, 4 AH-1W Super Cobra helicopters

Ship's company:
82 officers, 882 enlisted, and 1,900+ Marines

Armament:
2 rolling airframe missile launchers, 2 Phalanx Close-In Weapons Systems, 3 50-caliber machine guns, 4 25-millimeter MK 38 machine guns

Commissioning date, first ship:
1975

CHAPTER TWO

AMPHIBIOUS ASSAULT SHIP CHARACTERISTICS

The dominant feature of an amphibious assault ship, like that of an aircraft carrier, is its long, broad, flat deck, 844 feet (257 meters) **bow** to **stern**. But there's far more to the ship, like the **superstructure**. The superstructure rises like a small, 15-story castle from the flight deck. Within it is the ship's command and control center with its sophisticated electronic systems.

One of the most interesting—and functional—features of a big assault ship is the well deck, or docking well. The well deck is like a giant pool under the flight deck. In the *Wasp* class, the well deck is 266 feet (81 meters) long and about 49 feet (15 meters) wide. Landing craft are launched from the well deck.

FACT FILE ★

SAILORS DON'T NORMALLY WELCOME THE IDEA OF A SHIP TAKING ON WATER. WELL DECK WATER, HOWEVER, DOES NOT SINK THE SHIP BECAUSE IT'S LIMITED TO A RELATIVELY SMALL, CONTAINED AREA. IT'S NOT REALLY A "HOLE IN THE BOAT."

▲

The Kearsarge *superstructure rises above its flat flight deck. An AV-8B Harrier (foreground) is parked while another approaches for landing.*

▲

A Navy lieutenant commander directs aircraft from his perch at primary control in the tower of the amphibious assault ship USS Saipan.

By taking on seawater in its **ballast** tanks, an amphibious assault ship increases its weight and lowers its stern. Seawater rushes into the well deck compartment when the stern gate is opened. Landing craft are shuttled by elevator into the "pool" and then motor directly through the open gate to the ocean and onward. By forcing water from its ballast tanks, the ship lightens, the stern rises, and well tank water empties out.

The newest landing craft is the remarkable LCAC. Like other hovercraft, it literally flies—on a cushion of air it manufactures with four fans driven by gas turbine engines. The air is trapped in a rubberized canvas "skirt." The entire hull of the 88-foot (27-meter) long LCAC rides about 4 feet (1.3 meters) above the water.

FACT FILE ★

THINK YOU'D LIKE AN LCAC TO DASH ABOUT TOWN, OR DART OFF TO THE NEAREST LAKE? WHILE AIR-CUSHIONED LANDING CRAFT HAVE GREAT APPEAL FOR THEIR ABILITY TO SPEED HEAVY LOADS TO A LANDING SITE, THEY REQUIRE A HIGHLY SKILLED PILOT. AN LCAC NEEDS 1,500 FEET (457 METERS) TO STOP AND MORE THAN 6,000 FEET (1,829 METERS) FOR A FULL TURN.

An LCU (Landing Craft Utility) maneuvers into
position to enter the well deck of the amphibious
assault ship Saipan. At the time of this photograph
in 2005, Saipan was engaged in humanitarian
assistance efforts to Haiti.

▲

The LCAC is a high-speed hovercraft that rides on a cushion of air engineered by the craft itself and is trapped in a rubberized "skirt."

The LCAC can carry more than 60 tons (54.6 metric tons) at over 40 knots (46 miles, 74 kilometers per hour). It can haul people, weapons, cargo, and vehicles, including an M-1 tank. It can even travel inland and clear obstacles up to 4 feet (1.3 meters) high. Trucks and track vehicles can exit quickly from ramps at each end.

The *Wasp*-class ships have two aircraft elevators and six cargo elevators. They transport material from storage holds throughout the ship to the flight deck, hangar bay, and vehicle storage area.

Amphibs carry a variety of aircraft. The mix typically includes 23 helicopters and 6 AV-8B Marine Harrier jets. Harriers are designed to attack and destroy surface and air targets, to escort helicopters, and to take on other duties as required. Harriers are V/STOL (Vertical/Short Takeoff and Land) attack jets. They can take off on a short runway, making them ideal for the relatively short decks of amphibs.

▲

An AV-8B Harrier makes a final approach to the amphibious assault ship Saipan.

▲

Aboard the amphibious assault ship Kearsarge, *crew members upload a Sea Sparrow missile into a launcher cell.*

Because they may operate close to battle, amphibious assault ships are equipped like the best clinics. The *Wasp* class has 600 hospital beds and 6 operating rooms. The only American warships with larger hospital care facilities are the true hospital ships.

An amphibious assault ship's weapons include machine guns, 20-millimeter guns, two Sea Sparrow missile launchers, and two rolling airframe missile (RAM) launchers for defense against anti-ship missiles.

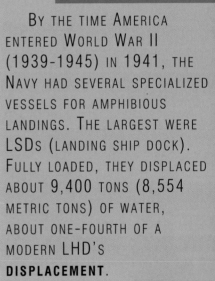

FACT FILE ★

BY THE TIME AMERICA ENTERED WORLD WAR II (1939-1945) IN 1941, THE NAVY HAD SEVERAL SPECIALIZED VESSELS FOR AMPHIBIOUS LANDINGS. THE LARGEST WERE LSDs (LANDING SHIP DOCK). FULLY LOADED, THEY DISPLACED ABOUT 9,400 TONS (8,554 METRIC TONS) OF WATER, ABOUT ONE-FOURTH OF A MODERN LHD's **DISPLACEMENT**.

CHAPTER THREE

EARLY HISTORY AND WORLD WAR II

U.S. military forces have a long, heroic history of amphibious landings in faraway places like Iwo Jima, Tarawa, Normandy, and Inchon. The know-how for those invasions began to take shape in the 1930s when U.S. Marines made shore landings several times during conflicts in Central and South America. Those events prompted the Navy to design specialized vessels for amphibious warfare.

The Navy and Marines used a variety of amphibious vessels during World War II. Perhaps the best known were the LSTs (landing ship tank), each nearly the length of a football field and displacing nearly 1,500 tons (1,365 metric tons).

Amphibious landing craft put Marines ashore on the sands of Iwo Jima on January 1, 1945, as U.S. forces, island by island, moved closer to Japan.

Manned by U.S. Coast Guard crews, LSTs open their jaws and release Marines in the surf of Leyte in October, 1944.

American Marine and, to a lesser extent, Army forces made amphibious landings in Europe and on several Japanese-held islands in the Pacific. Generally, ships carried the troops from port to a gathering place close to the assault site. There the troops would leave the transport ships to be ferried ashore by smaller landing craft.

Slow and only lightly armed, American landing vessels were sometimes easy targets for enemy guns. More than 100 were destroyed in World War II combat.

After World War II

CHAPTER FOUR

By the 1950s the Navy had a great respect for a relatively new type of aircraft—helicopters. At the same time, the Navy wanted to improve its ability to put Marines ashore. It wed the Marines with helicopters and improved its amphibious warfare capability by designing a new type of ship, the amphibious assault ship. The USS *Iwo Jima* (LPH 2), commissioned in 1961, was the first amphibious assault ship designed for that purpose. It could carry 25 helicopters and more than 1,500 Marines. The last of the seven *Iwo Jima*-class ships were retired in the mid-1990s.

▲

The amphibious assault ship linked U.S. Marine assaults with helicopters, like the CH-53E heavy-duty Marine Super Stallion shown here.

▲

Tarawa-class LHAs and their aircraft have been active in Middle East combat and in various humanitarian missions.

Three LHAs were active during Operations Desert Shield and Desert Storm in the Middle East. Since that time, LHAs and LHDs have been involved in additional action, including combat operations and **humanitarian** work. In recent years, American amphibious assault ships have been in combat zones near Kosovo, Iraq, and Afghanistan.

THE FUTURE OF AMPHIBIOUS ASSAULT SHIPS

CHAPTER FIVE

The next step in the development of big deck amphibs is a proposed 921-foot (281-meter) long ship that would support the Marine Corps's future jet fighter—the F-35B Joint Strike Fighter—and the MV-22 Osprey aircraft. The new ship, designated LHA(R), would also add vehicle and cargo stowage room and upgraded electronics. It's planned for delivery in 2013.

Both the F-35B and the tilt-rotor Osprey, which can take off and land like a helicopter, are expected to be operational early this century. Meanwhile, some of the *Tarawa*-class ships are scheduled to remain in service until at least 2015. The *Wasp*-class ships should be in service well into the 2030s.

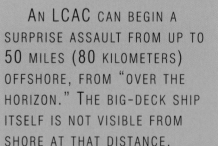

FACT FILE ★

AN LCAC CAN BEGIN A SURPRISE ASSAULT FROM UP TO 50 MILES (80 KILOMETERS) OFFSHORE, FROM "OVER THE HORIZON." THE BIG-DECK SHIP ITSELF IS NOT VISIBLE FROM SHORE AT THAT DISTANCE.

▲

V-22 Osprey tilt-rotor vertical/short takeoff and landing (VSTOL) aircraft practice close-in maneuvers aboard the Wasp-*class USS* Iwo Jima.

▲

The Wasp-*class* Bonhomme Richard *and other amphibious assault ships in its class are planned for active service well into the 2030s.*

GLOSSARY

amphibious (am FIB ee us) — capable of existing on both land and in water

ballast (BAL ust) — a heavy substance used to improve stability or control the weight of a ship

bow (BAU) — the front part of a ship

classes (KLAS uz) — groups of ships manufactured to the same, or very similar, specifications, such as the *Wasp* class of American amphibious assault ships

commissioning (kuh MISH un ing) — the act of officially placing a ship into U.S. Navy service

cruisers (KRU zurz) — heavily armed warships, smaller than battleships, and, in recent times, armed with guided missiles

destroyers (duh STROI urz) — surface warships traditionally used to defend larger, slower ships from submarines (modern destroyers are armed with guided missiles for multi-missions)

displacement (dis PLAY smunt) — the water displaced by a floating ship; the tonnage of the water displaced

frigates (FRIG utz) — surface warships, smaller than cruisers and destroyers, armed with guided missiles

hull (HUL) — the main frame and body of a ship

humanitarian (hyu MAN uh ter ee un) — that which is done to help people in need

stern (STURN) — the rear part of a ship

superstructure (SOO pur STRUK chur) — the major structure or structures built onto and rising above a ship's upper deck

well deck (WEL DEK) — a controlled water area under an amphibious assault ship's flight deck. Landing craft can be launched from the well deck.

INDEX

FURTHER READING

Green, Michael. Amphibious Ships. Capstone, 1999

McGowen, Tom. *Assault from the Sea: Amphibious Invasions of the 20th Century*. Lerner, 2002

WEBSITES TO VISIT

http://www.chinfo.navy.mil/navpalib/factfile/ships/ship-lha.html

http://navysite.de/ships/lha.htm

ABOUT THE AUTHOR

Lynn M. Stone is the author and photographer of many children's books. Lynn is a former teacher who travels worldwide to pursue his varied interests.

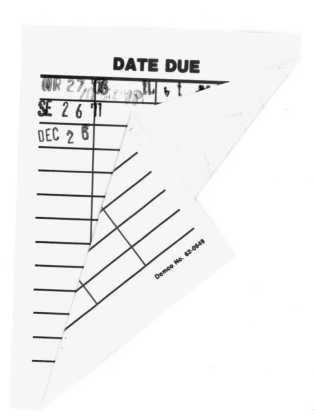

DATE DUE

MR 27 06

SE 2 6 11

DEC 2 6

Demco No. 62-0549